CW01149622

If Eyes Could Talk

Written and Illustrated by Alayna Robertson

Copyright © 2024 Alayna Robertson

All Rights Reserved.

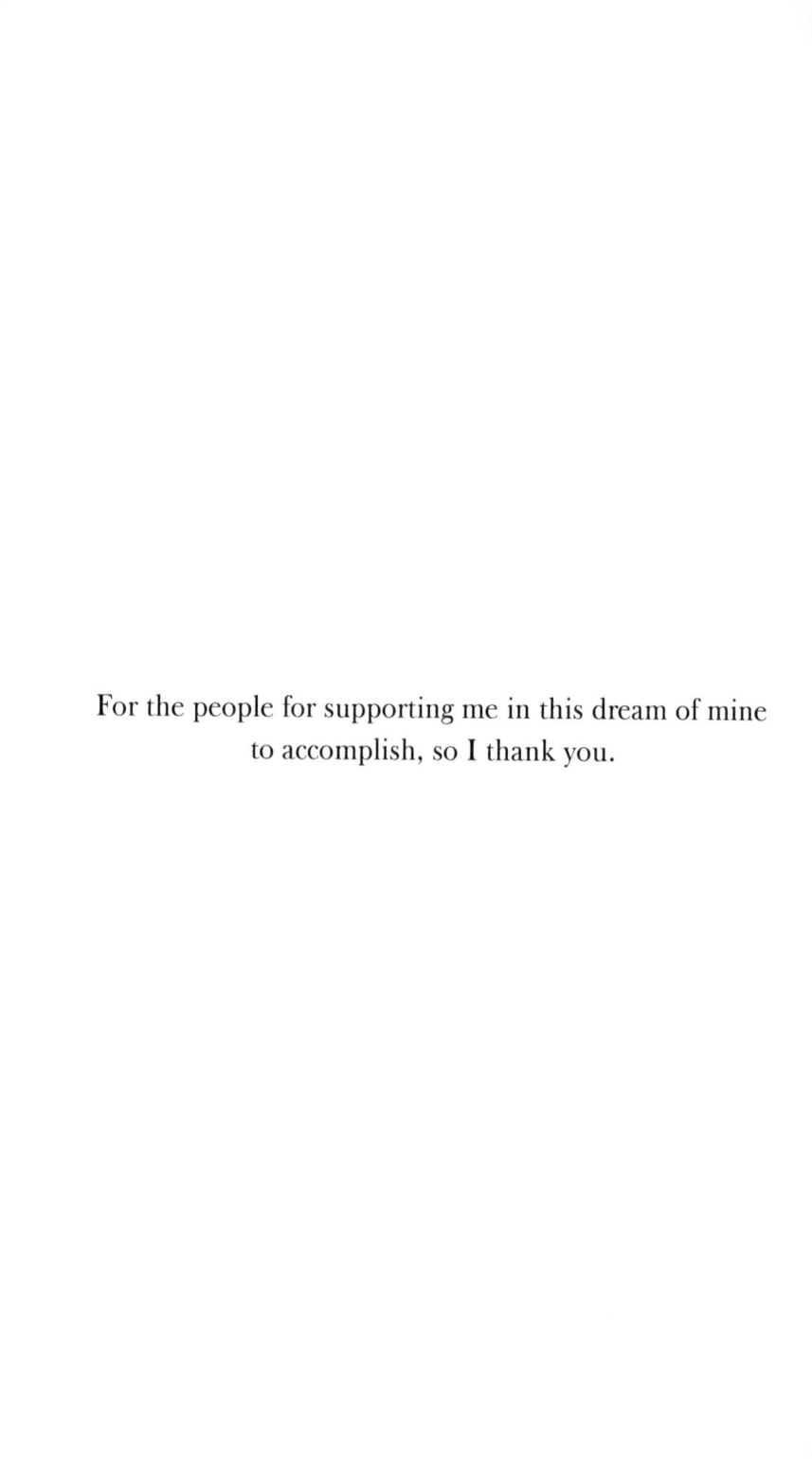

For the people for supporting me in this dream of mine to accomplish, so I thank you.

Contents

1. Hidden Treasure
2. Pearly Gates
3. The Shell and Pointy ears
4. Worn Hands
5. Hazel Eyes
6. Warriors and Bulldogs
7. Heads Spinning
8. Someone to Swing with
9. Empty Bed
10. Cry for Freedom
11. Pot Overblown
12. One more Bite
13. Hard Stomps
14. Mood Ring
15. Still Stands
16. Mummy's Perfume
17. Magnolia Petals
18. Super Suit
19. Disposable Memories
20. Statue of Us
21. Signed and Undelivered
22. You're Back
23. Mistletoe
24. Wasted Capability
25. The original Mrs. Parks
26. Nasal Drip
27. Beautiful Being
28. Mother Earth
29. Under the Bedsheets of Blues
30. Stitches of the Quilt cloth
31. Unknown Security Guard
32. Noah's House
33. Wine and Dine
34. Blue Heart not, Red
35. Mi Amour
36. Miss. Sweet Treats
37. The Refraction is Forming
38. Last Note
39. Powdered Sugar
40. Extra Smooth
41. On the Midnight Train to me
42. Children of the Carrie
43. The Inevitable Picture
44. Sixteen and Counting
45. Pretty and Improper
46. Outside of the Gate
47. Rare Find
48. Barbies and Beyblades
49. Wilting Flower
50. Slow Dancing
51. The Sweetest Blessing
52. Eyes Open
53. Twiddling one's Thumbs
54. The Green Ladies
55. Suga Mama and Baby Boy
56. Rotten Teeth
57. Overrated
58. Mrs. Thompson's Class
59. Brown Sugar
60. Old strings Attached
61. Generational Downfall
62. One pound and Three Ounces
63. Keeping my fingers Crossed
64. Just Genes
65. Can't you See
66. Thank you "this" Much

Introduction

I have been writing songs, poems, short stories, and everything since I was a young girl. The library has been and will always be my safe space to reside in.

I love reading and writing about real things. I think when reality is at play; it makes me more comfortable to see that everything isn't a fantasy that people try to make it out to be.

I want this poetry book to open people up about life and see what they are glossing over within their own lives through these poems and of course to have a gasp, wow, and laugh in between.

This poetry book is for people who need someone to relate to and see that they are not alone.
Let this be a book of perspective in a creative way that you can understand. This is poetry is about the light and darkness of life.

I hope you enjoy.

Hidden Treasure

Your map plan is written in the stars for you, as slaves to the north star trying to be freed.

It has markings that are invisible in plain sight.
Jewels hidden in the dirt, waiting for you to find it.

You're being unheard and your bed is cold at night and all you see is grey, wishing for a story you never thought would be real. Anything you want to happen can come true.

The terms will alter to be for your best growth because God already has your story published. You just need to read it.

Pearly Gates

Luminescence circulates into my body.

Vibrations of ecstasy rush in my veins as you look into my eyes and see my journey.

A window opens to bring you my love.
Joy, I speak with my words and have a longing as I search within my heart.

This connection stretches as strings for thousands of years so far that none can even see.

Up above, I see you patiently waiting for me to bring you near me someday.

The Shell and Pointy Ears

The race starts, and you hit the ground running in life. Full of passion and belief to keep the pace to move ahead as your score gets higher. Goals are set and stars appear to dream upon.

Other records are being broken and set. They are finished before you're prepared to go. Waiting for the next feeling rested as they look back at your game with questions. Lagging and out of breath stuck in the rut of hitting that wall.

Trying not to go too fast just to impress the crowd that's staring down at you. But going as you can handle to cross that line for yourself. Focused and timed exactly for your wins, and only your path to walk in.

No matter what jersey you wear or how nice your sneakers are. Just playing your game in life can be the best achievement and trophies can offer.

Worn Hands

Fury strikes as a blade, a swift motion goes through me. I shake with tension in my colored eyes that burns like fire in my chest.

Pain and sadness pour to the roots bursting within the ground as a rocket into space. So freely it flies, can't control it within my grasp. I'm tied down and don't know how to numb the sparks.

All I have were the shoes on my sore feet and the glitter of brightness left from the rush of blackness inside and out of me. I leave footsteps behind as I go towards something real.

Hazel Eyes

Yellow, blue, and green come out of my fingertips with smoothness and precision.

In the air, steps crowd around the room with stories to tell.

Warmth overflows the soul in my heart, and smoke and laughter mix into the voices with a sweet melody.

How I will never forget that moment and desire for its return.

Warriors and Bulldogs

We see cold glossy floors, lower lockers, and C list food that turns into stomach aches.

From bratty cliques to anime and rainbow hair that comes all around me as to phones and ugly fights.

School plays, cringy assemblies, and two-faced friends give off peer pressure and mirror pictures that come on our screens for the naïve to follow along.

Weights lift off our shoulders when that cap flutters in the air as you wonder which path is the right one to take.

Making sure the last four years were the right ones to look happy upon. You want to look back, wishing that tried harder.

Heads Spinning

Funny moods you express with no love or happiness.
Your love spins like a carousel. I fell. Up and down it makes me sick because you just don't know how to quit.

I follow your road to take, then I fall and break.
Can't confide, I hide and put on roles just to make it through the day. I'm always afraid and don't know what to say.

In the end, we still stand together hand in hand, cold as the last woman you but in your trance.
Trying to give just once more glance. Fighting to be out of the cycle dance. Maybe I missed my last chance.

Someone to Swing with

They taught me how to pray, to trust when the world is wearing a colored changing mask.

The lonely child, alone with no one to hold but that inner voice. Never been seen, rubble chips away at her.

A familiar warmth surrounds her with open arms, holding out their hands for a lifetime of friendship for me to take.

Jumping so high up in the sky looking at myself seeing I'm truly starting to fly.

Empty Bed

That night I was standing all alone wishing you were here while I was cold as stone.

Tossing and turning can't keep my eyes open. I'm broken to see you leave, saying that there's nothing left for me.

Nothing makes me feel as you do. It's true. Forever, you will always be the only one. Our time has quickly come.

Can't be the same again, you said "Hey we can be just friends".

Cry for Freedom

Pretending can clog the mind.
Suppressing under that unseen
appearance no one has graced their eyes
upon.

Parts of their persona shine through the
walls, fiercely it starts to crack and break,
urging to be released out of its dark spell
into the wild.

They wonder if this slow shift will ever
facilitate or even be a question to be
answered.
There is congestion on the polar sides of
destruction.

Dreaming to see a reflection of the days
that their screams behind that glass
bubble will shatter and prayers will be
understood and seen.

Pot Overblown

Blood boils up high in me.
Seeing you so quiet and
down hurts me and makes
me bite bricks.

Anxiety mixes into tears
and rises to break knuckles.
Soaking it up like a sponge
in the sea, waves start
crashing against the coast.
Havoc and mayhem go
through my mind, swirling
with thoughts.

Dark clouds with red
strikes of lightning come
with power in my hands.
I'm strong. Nothing can
make me see differently.

I look down on what's
hurting you and what's
coming for them will be the
sentence they were meant
to have through my eyes.

One more Bite

One last time, they say. The tough urge that's inside of them overspills with dissatisfaction and regret. After each promise gets broken, shame drowns inside one's mind.

Fighting in a crowd of temptation, dark voices bomb their composure and trick them to the other side of the corrupt game.

Their cage is open, but they still choose to wear the veil they made for themselves and go back one last time.

Hard Stomps

Stained red all over my bed.
Spunky spinning heads come from the dead.
Where should I be instead?
Am I being misread?
Treading lightly towards the door.
Chest burning inside.
Where should I hide?
Walls to wall dripping with my pride.
I close my eyes and I see thunder and rain.
Does my pain have to be explained?
Streets with no laughter.
Who can I come after with my disasters?
Hands over your mouth as you struggle and I come from behind.
You will always be blind.
My crimes will forever be burned in your mind.

Mood Ring

Blackmail is the face of the wolf.
Your secrets were told into lies
as they were cut from behind.

The monster vanishes into the
dark. Black and blue bruises are
on your spirit.

But scars can be treated, time is
patience, and hurt can be
forgiven if wanting to be truly
set free from the monster in
your closet.

Still Stands

Your love echoes as the heart remains.

Endless land of possibilities and colors blend into clarity. Eyes look like butterflies of hope fluttering in a field of dreams.

Shine beams brightly through you as you come to me with the will of all that glows from your soul.

Your love pours out and feeds the plan to be fruitful.

Night water breaks and your joy sprinkles in the sky like shining stars.

Invisible, though your heart will always be held. You've never left as we're meant to be.

Mummy's Perfume

Forgotten closets bring missing buttons,
fur coats, old China, needle cushions,
tattered tulle dresses, and gold crosses.

Shattered glasses, leather bibles, boxes
full of hospital tags, and polarized cake
face birthday parties.

Diary entries from 95' and shared
vacations of our time on the pillowed
beach. Empty purple pumps, acid denim
jackets, and antique wedding albums
clutter the space.

Rushing with fevered emotions, the
checklist still will be completed and
rooms to be unburdened.

Sweeping away the dust of the
memories, doors will close and be
thought of in the past so new ones can
be free to be born.

Magnolia Petals

Blades of grass comb through my toes as I
walk through the troubles of history.
Willow trees sing in the holy sun as it
kisses my face to know life is here.

Bricks and bones coward in the cold
corner to be ashamed of the black and blue
it's caused.

Breaths are taken and released into an
open world of wonders. Sipping frosted
tea, swinging to blues that softly tickle my
ears with love.

The fog disappears over the airy mire and
chills dance down my spine.
As motion slows down, eyes shut to the
calm children's laughter. Sheets of cotton
gently caress my mahogany flesh.

Scents of sweetness cloud the room and
hug me so gently. A serene state of mind is
present as I sleep in the sounds of the
south.

Super Suit

When I left, you kept changing behind my back. You didn't think about how I felt when you took a different way to walk.

Didn't care if the door was closed on me and if I could get out the door. You can't win the game I played on you. I lure you into my house of mirrors.

The reflection will never change how I see and what you will be. I didn't get the golden prize to go with the crown on my head that I said was promised to me.

You will never find another superhero like me again. Even though my disguise has been shown, all this time I'm just another number waiting for my entitled victory.

Disposable Memories

I stare at a blank wall with empty holes in it wondering what to distract myself next.

What can I hang up to block up the fading picture of what I thought was forever?

Turn around and tell me your fantasy isn't fading too, so I can believe for a second.

Tell me you can still smell the sweet flowers in our room once and that those whispers aren't just a lost voice to be forgotten.

Closing my eyes, I see our old picture once on the wall becoming covered with Mrs. Someone new.

Guess you took the picture out that came with the frame.

Statue of Us

Lights shine as bright as the tall sky I see above me.

Rugged textures of culture surround me with scents of home cooking and mixed emotions. Urgent footsteps stomp and step forward to see what the next big thing is to be.

Alleys connect with the street corners to lay out history's past as stepping stones for the black, white, yellow, and brown to melt together as crayons on a hot July afternoon.

Day to day and night to night, the city never wastes a day for anything and everything to happen, always making it for all eyes to see.

Signed and Undelivered

I wrote you a letter hidden in my mind.
Telling you how I feel and what my dreams are as I look at the moonlight through my window night after night.

That letter will collect dust because you haven't opened the seal to my heart's desire.

You have the key to my world.
Maybe you already know what my letter says because you have one that matches mine.

Scared if it's written in red ink or not, maybe one day I'll send out my 4-page letter.

You're Back

I almost lost you.
I was in a maze and I couldn't
find the way out.
My grip was weak on your
presence.

Sorrowfully ask others to help
search for my missing person.
You didn't read the message I left
for you to hear.

I look back and see you and then
again, you're gone once more.

You stand around the corner
waiting to answer what I have to
say.
Where were you last winter when
I needed you?
It's too late to put the picture
together since the frame has been
damaged and glass has shattered
everywhere. So sharp it would cut
a hand if touched.

You haunt me now with your
attendance as you hold me tight to
tell me you never left.

Mistletoe

How much longer do you think I will have to wait to open my present?

Has the man forgotten about me?
Was there something important to get to, maybe the better kids first?

Or will I just get another knockoff I didn't ask for and it gets tossed in the closet like the others?

Foggy and blurred as I'm in a snow globe waiting for the snow to clear and to see the light at the end of the path.

In a way, it hurts me to see that there is no present under the tree for me.
Thinking that Santa never got my letter for this one thing I wanted.

I can't hear, see, or touch what it will be like when my eyes meet this special present.

One day I'll walk down the stairs with excitement, seeing it under the tree for me ready to open and have it as I deserve it to be all mine.

Wasted Capability

I saw fake potential in you, something deep down that I know nobody sees.
A part of you that I know you try to be.

It hurts you for anyone to watch the lonely game you truly play.
The true winner has the sight now, you know you're not the prize to praise now.

How? I know comes to you in your mind why your artificial light has died.

Children can only play for so long, hang up the kiddy shoes that are wrong to be on.

Who is going to love you when the makeup comes off and the tears of a clown falls down?
Definitely not me.

The original Mrs. Parks

Secret whispers spout like fire and thunder to the masses.
Our differences in darkness cover us like skin.

Names strike like pointed swords so our kids can watch.
Can't sit in the empty seat that's never been reserved for you and me.

Faced as black rubble on the street, their shiny shoes walk over us intently.
As salt to a snail, gun in hand, and injustice to be brushed away and stored in lost files.

Their tone is angry.

Their language is too coarse.

Not abundant enough to be profitable for blue-eyes.
Too adequate to fight against the brick wall that won't come down to see what can be.

We must fully embrace who we are and go against the fear of speaking about what's happening behind the curtain of reality.

Nasal Drip

Winter has gone and the past still stays frozen on your lips.

Numb limbs stiffen your ways and have left you with none of the sun's warmth.

Spring transit breaks the hard core deep inside to see life forming in front of your eyes.

Seeds are planted and forgotten in the ground and begin living for the first time.

The solstice of the heat burns for a million flames. A passion to be the best and different from the rest.

Seasons aren't a lifetime and those allergies will go away with every spray and then and only then you will breathe again.

Beautiful Being

The sun rises and sets to your smile.
As waves caress the smooth sands as do to your touch.

Roses blush in your presence when they meet your eyes.
Your words make trees stronger with every breath taken.

I feel your love when you are not here. It's the sweetest thing I will ever have.

You're the gift God has given me.
The world treasure is the mind you carry.
This is the best secret kept.

Mother Earth

I have a tree in my yard. I want you to meet.

This tree has been growing with me for as long as I remember.
It's always there for me to give me shade and protect me from the harsh sun of the world.

It can give surprises that drop on me sometimes, but I know that's natural with trees.

It springs fruits of its labor that make it so sweet to treasure. It gives the gloomy days a spark of joy when I need it.

These branches are all in different forms from their time in my yard. Some branches have strong leaves, and some have died and grown into beautiful flowers.

These roots have not stopped their cycle. Water runs through it to keep on shining for the next morning.

I'm proud of this tree being grounded for me. When thunder and lightning are trying to strike it down, and there's damage being done, It's always healing, even when scars can be seen.

Winds blow through this tree, it feels like an elevated breeze. I know it feels my love without saying a word.

Under the Bedsheets of Blues

I feel infinite as we float so lightly to Chopin's prelude.

Looking into your spearing, sparkling eyes makes me melt as butter on pancakes and you're the syrup on top that makes it so delicious to eat.

Never thought this would happen to me.

Night owls never sleep till the morning but you woke me up so gently, I couldn't resist.

You looked inside me, something that nobody else has tried to see. You read my pages and not just the cover of who I am.

So open and free as the wind came beneath my wings for the first time. You make me fly so high I touch the stars that were lined out for us. You shine so brightly every time I see you; it hurts to look at something so divine.

This music was written just for us, as were the only ones dancing and could hear how beautiful this truly sounds.

Stitches of the Quilt Cloth

There's a rip on the cloth of the world.

Appearance can seem ugly to others and the rest see it with culture, a service of fluidity in its different texture, which is beautiful to thy human.

Confusion with anger is as sour as a sharp tongue. Indoctrination being taught from the past remains in its repeating cycle.

When is it the time for the clothes to finally dry and be laid to rest?

Doesn't seem to be the right color for where its patch needs to be. Does it turn everything red? Or is it just their hands?

Riots die out and result in broken windows. Speeches go off into dusty books as they pass from its sight and never be brought up to when the bell rings.

Wars cry out in damaged flags, homes break down into tears and crumble at the lost joy we once had.

Feeling karma being set on fire to our land for being the black sheep. To get sold for our wool and kicked out into the cold to be used for meat later.

An urgency needs to be voiced for the children's laceration. That there is a way to change and control within. We're all bonded together as grass to the earth and blood to our bodies. Don't let its obsolescent be the winner in our match to fight back.

Unknown Security Guard

Swirling destruction is my cyclone storm. Objects thrown at me coming from left and right, breaking me down like a collapsing house, so open with nothing around it to see it fall.

Riding through a tunnel, my engine starts and stops. It stalls every morning as I free my eyes to see the same blank wall in sequence. Work and no play kill me daily trying to find something fulfilling.

Luminant edges go towards the end of the road. There you were with both hands waiting at the end for me to come out safe and in one piece.

Noah's House

Many rooms crowd with little toes
running all over the place and paint
prints on the walls.
Wrap-around porches with scratches from
your little handy projects as you lock back
at your accomplishment.

A special place just for my colorful mind
to create our future in.
Home-cooked meals to help the hungry
bellies after a hard works day to be
fulfilled with my sweet sauce.

Arguments over wet countertops and
calling it an "entertainment room" come
every Saturday afternoon with you and
me.

Bubble baths and basement parties can be
our secret not to tell.
Dreams come from this place I have with
you.
You're my real home and will always stay.

Wine and Dine

Deep beats pulse through your hurting feet with hot spices burning your nose. Watery eyes see nationalizes permeate the land all over.

Feathers of the island float in the smoky air and glittery skin bathes in the luminary moonlight as it never stops circulating with its sensual groove.

The soca sounds shock the brain just as your tongue does after each "last" sip of that special red punch concoction.

Lovers meet, and connection finds its way back to its roots of your ancestors' old beach houses.

Red and black paint represents the warrior marks when going into the streets of the fun and unexpected.

A strong steel band plays to stimulate the fast dance all day and night. Hard church bells play in the morning after your next hangover rings in your head, wishing for it to stop.

This internal party never sleeps because whatever happens in carnival, stays in carnival.

Blue Heart not, Red

Guns fall and you run for cover in the wet park. Being scared out of sagging shorts you try to fit in looking at what you lost.

Tried to love your soft eyes but couldn't see past the colored bandanna you always wore.

Closing off to the world as you walk to the unlit cell that slowly brings your spirit down.

Needles, smoke, and broken in-store alarms fill your mind and soul as time gives you one last chance for you to have.

Small towns and dirty minds think alike even when wanting to be washed clean of their mistakes and scene getaways.

Saying you're sorry wasn't something I wanted to hear.

Angry words scared the inner child on that holy night. All that was said was very clear, crystal. Just like the one you stole from me.

But sunshine always comes through the dark house you sleep in and a new day can change everything.

Mi Amour

Hold me forever in your love.
As I long for you always, waiting till the day to see you.

Days, months to years pass by and I still wait for the rainy day I hear your knock at my door.

Rose petals fall off as another day comes without you near me to touch.
Please free me from my slumber and make me have my happily ever after.

Make our hearts drench in each other's being.
You are the music box I'll listen to for eternity, as I can't be without you.

You fulfill me in my dreams, as that's all I have. Memories that have never been but only in a different world.
Tonight still stands as I still dream of you, hoping you see me in yours.

Miss. Sweet Treats

Single lady, don't you see me calling you?

Baby, the way you walk around drives me crazy.

Thinking about you so much latcly, can't you give me your love tonight?

I don't want to fight. Let's make the moment count all night.

I got my ride. I'll take you anywhere you'd like.

Come and shake my tree. Meet me in the back seat because it will all be so pleasing to me.

You're the beauty queen I see, someone they all want to be.

Being friends just ain't enough for me,

Guys stop and stare, but I'm the one who cares.

Run a thousand miles just to hear you say you'll be with me. I know you don't see.

I'm more than any man you can comprehend. I'm bigger than all of them times ten.

I'll paint your picture so you can last longer. Don't ponder.

My love will be the strongest, my heart will always grow fonder.

Chocolate tastes so sweet as it swirls in my mind like a sweet treat.

Oh baby, just let me be every greedy desire and I know you won't say that I don't burn your fire.

The Refraction is Forming

I'm done being a pinata.

I'm done being the one with all the secret sweets.

I'm done saying nobody's home.

I'm done with everybody not seeing how much you love me in the dark.

My house is full of rainbow expectations that need to be addressed.

Everybody is going to see the sparkles shine when it comes to us.

Are you ready? My bags have been packed since June and I'm eager to start over.

Maybe it's just Cher and cologne getting to me for the thousandth time.

So tell me now what you want to say to the plain crowd because my colorful self is going crazy.

Last Note

These soft keys of ivory give infinite freedom and depth of emotional expression to you and your ears.

It brings light to your feet and breathes out your voice. Beats hum through your body, darkness, and sparks of color bleed out as to a light tune in your mind.

This joy rushes within you to last a lifetime. So cherish the music that leads to the Ladder.

Powdered Sugar

Groovy Late nights and coffee in
the morning come in like
daydreams. Pinch me or am I
bursting at the seams?

Seeing you there warms my heart as
I ask for you to stay longer.
You work nights now, but no name
tag is to be seen. You're looking
green, and maybe I need to
intervene.

Bathroom meetings on your lips
are the special on your daily menu.
I see you're making new friends in
and out of your "work" venue.

Deep down, I ask myself what I am
doing.
My love is still strong and overflows
with an urge for us to succeed.
Is it me or do you just want a taste
of that secret speed?

Don't know which way to go as I
walk down the street hoping I don't
see you asking for a "need".

Extra Smooth

I saw you tonight when you hid behind
the pillars, acting like you were
invisible.

It's been a month and you're wondering
if I'm still miserable.

Random drunk kisses with the blonde
on the right as you try to act like 5'5 is
tall.

While I'm questioning your actions,
trying to make a confused sense of it all.

Suggestions of strawberries and a scene,
as if that's what you think she wants to
do.

Can I be your new boo you ask,
standing with your dudes as you take
back another brew.

I think to myself, try not to choke on
the strawberry wine coolers this time,
 as walk out the door.
I guess you forgot what you swore but
that's what you get when you invest with
an incompetent chore.

On the Midnight Train to me

Your Assignment is finished.

I'm moving on to the new class of my life.

You haven't noticed the tired looks and distress.

Unresponsive texts you can't even see what's next from the invisible empress.

Funny faces cover the loneliness when I'm blue.

I've been here but you say nice to meet you.

Crybaby I am at night when the medicine wears off, I
stepping out the door when you sleep.

Could have been so perfect for you and me but you're just a creep.

I need to finally rest now and be who I'm meant to be.
Blindsided eyes have been washed with foresight of the wakened sea.

Children of the Carrie

I tried to heal your stabbed heart,

but blood was getting sucked out of me, as vampires do to anyone of substance.

I tried to be your friend when you cried in your coffin at night,

a part of me lost one's life just as you did long ago.

Listening to your screeching songs makes it uncomfortable to hear as blood pours down my skin.

Maybe I said things I shouldn't have, but it's hard when you are trying to be bitten by the unknown and the energy penetrates your light with each passing day.

I knew you needed someone to hold, and deep down I knew I shouldn't have opened your blackmail letter that was written in invisible ink.

Lies and secrets spread so quickly as wheat to a flame and I'm the one being burned at the stake for your perpetrating performance to the followers who believe your speech is real.

Piled up, waiting for the brick wall to fall as the truth steps out to be free once again.

Looking numb in people's eyes as I walk away, picturing myself in a straight jacket as if I'm the wrong one trying to be sent off and shamed to be gone.

Your shame was never mine. All is forgiven as they have all lived through lively innocent eyes at a point in time.

The Inevitable Picture

As I sleep at night, my visions picture Charlie Brown Christmases, hand-me-downs, and a scratched Hannah Montana CD in rotation.

The after-school Reba and Qubo TV come on by the spoonful as a mouth to peanut butter.

Small two bedroom apartments, forgotten community pools, and sharing a bed made everything feel so "grand" knowing you tried your best.

Latchkey till four as the DS battles build tension within the lunchroom, quaking to see the winner.

On back seat bus rides seeing the secrets of the students wondering why.

Note passing embarrassment to last a lifetime of spread as far as can see.

Thankfully, I woke up in time to see that it was all a past dream.

Sixteen and Counting

Scents of burnt icing spread in the air and the fog covers me when candles blow out to smoke.

I'm not winning the race fast enough for my competition as I sit at the head of the table. The technique is wrong and faces of disappointment swallows me in my mind.

But on the outside of my ring circus, the crowd is celebratory to see what my show has to offer. That the fool is a new year, starting over for another chapter and awaits my next move to wow the audience.

Pretty and Improper

Blind as moles and loud as monkeys, teachers scurry to tell mother their ideologues. They screech as vultures in a field waiting for me to be roadkill.

Bored with numbing information that won't be used when I can't afford the rent.

Candyland and therapists try to poke my mind as misdiagnosis is at play. Not trying to find my face under the mask I wear to the world.

Forced microphone presentations and arguments make the child cry at night with no one around to hear but Mr. Duck.
Certain classes are not needed but demanded to be taken.

Names of every kind are to be heard under the heinous undertone of the playground sun. She turns mute, swift but surely.

Closed off as test dividers, she sits in between wondering if trying makes a difference and if it will be the same as the cold chair in the corner that's waiting for her.

Gifted and bright is the girl indeed and within hidden armor she shines so brightly, while they pushed her hard into the ground as they tried to shut up the little girl in pigtails.

Outside of the Gate

You're seeing through the eyes of this child who's looking inside.

They live outside of town.

They've seen many things about what
they thought was over and dismissed it into the background.

Their special acceptance into town was different, struggling to find another way inside.

New openings do come along but crash and echo so loud that it is not to be forgotten. As the sound replays repeatedly, it becomes numb inside.

Outcast to the wave of people around them. Unaware of the power they hold as others just see a dark room they lie in at night.

Grew too fast to be understood, pushing and pushing till trying to be seen.

It's hard to explain, feeling there's no one completely the same.

Surviving not to live. Sunshine shines on this child throughout them. When alone there is another town to explore.

Rare Find

When our eyes locked, I recognized the soul of who you are. I saw your essence; I saw your heart.

As the energetic pull was coming closer as if we'd known each other for a thousand years. As Adam saw Eve, you're the urge I've been searching for.

We had a loss for words trying to feel if they were really real.
Now I see the face that I've loved for so long
I met my twin from my dreams that's been waiting to become a reality, to start a new beginning as being baptized once more.

Wanting to shed tears in my eyes as I cry out to my other half.
Hands greet with electricity and a smile of joy to seal the deal.
We're the gift we've been wishing to have to open and keep it forever close.

The spirit rushes through us and won't die.
Time stops and there's nobody else to see
that compares.

Darkness is around us as we shine bright as two stars in our own universe.
You knocked the breath out of my voice, and no words were to be spoken. Finally, I could exhale.

Barbies and Beyblades

Sparkly cheetah dresses and dream house collections galore fill the small space.

Hallway runways and play performances for the tired parents to see while we ask if they are paying attention.

Silly bands cutting off your circulation up to your elbow with pride.

Flip-flop sales cause broken toes just to get through the doors, as they are destroyed a month later.

Gospel music on Saturdays blasts the walls down, trying to fake my sleep off as Pine-Sol burn my nose hairs.

Trying to be a female Tony Hawk but have the balance of Mr.Bean with every failed attempt.

Book fairs don't compare to prom, not by a long shot so don't fight me on it.

Look through a child's eyes sometimes. You might have a peanut butter and jelly sandwich waiting for you with a note saying "I love you, and have a good day".

Wilting Flower

I had to drop you.

Kick rocks to you.

Try to stop me, can't be on top of me.

Don't make me pop off like New York.

You don't want this formidable work.

Rocks so hard it hurts your brain, forever in a dent, tragedy, ain't it?

Just charge it to the account, because it didn't count.

This can't be right as you've only got it for the clout and to talk about me around town, but look who's bowing to my crown.

Track all-Star right? Can't pass the bar, didn't even go that far.

Got my other paprika on the line, you wasted my time. Maybe you'll do better with her asinine mind.

Highly doubtful, it was so unimpactful.

Tried to make me playable,

bet you can even spell dishonorable.

As children with toys, now our playdate is over. So tired of these little boys.

Slow Dancing

I'm happy as the morning shine.

You're my jackpot prize.

Found that earth has angels and dreams do come true, blues no more to be seen, I am forever green.

Sweet as the ripened berries on a summer afternoon.

You shine as a light to a full moon.

Not fair for me to have all of this bliss of a kiss that never does miss.

Been so long since I touched a warm hand, coldness always touches my skin, but you feel like a sin that wins over and over again.

The Sweetest Blessing

Lullabies play as I watch you sleep in the soft bed I made for you tonight.

Thunderstorms and sick nights cower in the corner as I fight them off for you.

This is a love no one can match as heaven brought you down for me to have and cherish so tightly.

You shine bright every morning as I see you walk towards me to tell me about your dreams.

Your eyes are so pure of wonder and your cheeks are so kissable makes me never want to let you go.

You're my miracle, my one blessing that no one will understand. You're my gold at the end of the rainbow that I hold in my hand.

Our lasting love drops so deep that no one can't ever fathom to understand.

I'll always have these little moments to look back on. You cured my illness of loneliness. Your first smile was the medicine I needed.

My baby, you will always be.

Eyes Open

Coming up for that
breath as I take my
wash of holiness, elated
and light spreads
through my veins as I've
seen the world for the
first time.

People alike surround
me filled with love and
his spirit. A feeling of
heaven covers me like a
drop of sunlight in my
heart. A feeling I
strived to have again
and again.

But it quickly fades to
the past and opens me
up to see what the earth
is shown to be.

Twiddling one's Thumbs

I walk around in the beating sun to see luscious wonders around me.
Seeing beautiful wings fly so high to see things I ever wondered to grace upon someday.

I look at the sky and wonder why things change as they do and why trees have so many stories to tell.
Old bricks stack so tall for history to write itself on its walls.
Whose prestige shoes walked the same path as you and I do?

Looking at the past once shattered windows, inquisitive questions go through my brain asking,
what did the old poodle skirts have to do in that desk to make standards break?
What marches had to be taken for growth to sprout out and spread the word?

How did it feel to touch the skin of a snowy color in that crowd of revolution for the first time?
Did prosperity ever come true or are we just not living the "dream" that was spoken to us so many years ago?
You ask me.

The Green Ladies

Cackling in the other room doesn't make the walls soundproof.

Obscene words under your breath can't make it smell like flowers.

Frowns and faces are permement wrinkles waiting to say "hello there".

Pursed lips came untrendy when you followed along.

You're the OB. Be proud of the gauche stares.

Wicked cast the wrong actress because you would have excelled beautifully, Miss. Wang.

Curiosity killed the cow. Excuse me, the cat. Black in fact.

Rouge should be used instead of the green makeup that you try to pull off.

You better make sure you wake up early to take yourself out because the trash always says "wassup" on Tuesdays just for you, baby.

Suga Mama and Baby Boy

Breaking the ice once we walked in, everybody tripping with what were wearing as if their ensemble was not domineering.
People are all up in our space asking if he's mine, as if my ring ain't shining like gold mines. Make a blues man go blind.

On the sparkling floor in our world as our hands connect to the beats while we spin and twirl.
"You're such a cute little girl" In a flip tone, they speak.
Better but that beak away because it's getting in my drink.

Having a ball seeing that everyone doesn't want to miss it. While they hate from the other side of the rope wishing we would fall, look how they crawl such a shame in it all.

Dead when we leave the spot, look at you trying to drop it like it's hot.
You pop off like gunshots, making the other guys jealous since they're soft.

So excited to show you off looking like a hot boy summer.
Thank God for your mother.
Nobody can duplicate our stance. Others don't even stand a chance.

Rotten Teeth

How many sweets are you eating? Does that sugar high get you off?

Biting and leaving the scar that feeds you. Take all the gifts and not say thank you. Open it up and see what's really inside your box.
When the party is over and the last horn is blown, what do you have to give back?

What's the use of having your fork on everyone's plate when you have your piece of the dream in front of you?

Because eating too much can make you vomit and it's very real, nobody will want to clean it up for you. So start eating healthy or your engine will slowly burn out and go to the junkyard someday.

Overrated

Heart beds, nasty candy, kiddy cards, and overpriced flowers.

Reserved reservations weeks in advance, fluffy pillows, and candlelight tables.

I'm waiting for a call, checking back and forth at the screen, questioning where I should meet you.

Sitting alone on that red seat looking for your hand in the wave of people.

Agony and embarrassment I feel when they ask what's wrong.
Looking out the window the whole ride home, I say to myself, never again. Or so I thought.

Mrs. Thompsons Class

I remember when I heard you; I felt something I didn't believe was real.

Surprised that a kid could have such an aura, but found it so dazzling to see.

Mom laughs at the cute couple we would make.
So much in common as two friends and possibly wish to be more.

Too shy to tell each other what's really in our hearts, even though it's projected on the wall for our class to see.

It's the last day of school and I got told by your friend that you're looking for me to tell me something special.

But I never got to listen to your question as if that last bus ride was the answer. Seeing you go away forever and forgetting that I was even real.

Brown Sugar

Sweet like red juice, tight curls bounce like quarters off of you. Your definition speaks volumes as to a black pantheress in a cultural jungle.

You raise beautiful brown skin babies to the sun to be the future chain breakers of our reality. You're the warriors of the mission. Look under the roots of what we grow and see the real leaders of the afro tribe.

You're the shock of honey to the lips of society. You make them burn to crave each taste. They have a curiosity and an appetite for darkness, as so they should for the queens of the night.

Minds are sharp just as the heels you wear to make it rain day to night. You fly as rhythm and blues, which blissfully pour out and stick to people as you walk by.

When fire hits the flame, they run away from the real smoke that is your essence. You're the original headliner, others copy but can't remake your flow. It's cute to see, but they'll never be. Brown sugar is that spoonful that makes everything go down.

Old strings Attached

Dear You,
My moving boxes changed and opened to new spaces as I did that day. Not the same.
I brought you with me to this new home to live and be a unit that wouldn't break.

Still playing the role we needed to be in as everyone thoughtfully so, which they were right but deep down I knew it was wrong.

Fun times mask the deepness I wanted but couldn't find, trying not to waste any more time. Am I going to be fine with this change of mind?

Slowly drifting to another destination that doesn't have my name on it, an expired ticket is our way to go.
I know it's not your fault, we just need to be realized out of the vault.

Independent woman I am. I hope you understand, I know it hurts as it affects me too, but I do and always will still love you.
Love, me.

Generational Downfall

Get off that game and touch some grass for your feet to feel.
See that everything isn't just a virtual sonaro, comprendo?

Live in the real world and see what money feels like in your pocket. Do you wear a watch just for sport or can you tell time? Military or is it "I don't know it's not mine".

Dumb kids with screens hooked on the brain as we slowly drain. No mortals, no thy fellow man, no work to save one's life.

Why the pessimism ladies and gentlemen? No faith is seen through the grown. You don't think we cry? You probably don't even know why.

Why are we acting like rocks when we are gemstones waiting to be exposed? They see us as tramps, waiting for us to get hosed.

They think we are better off as cross and bones. Be leaders and not form into rows. We are so much more than we will ever know.
That was their time. Now it's our time for us to grow.

One Pound and Three Ounces

You're staring at a clear box,
knowing you are scared with
dread in your eyes.

Tears stream down your face as
if all your love has gone in one
split second.

On the edge, your pain collapses
on your stomach, moving
forward trying to reach out.

Oxygen tanks and asthma
attacks go hand in hand with
cold winters and hot summers.

Dreaming that I'm still a child,
that you have to protect me from
dangerous monsters under my
bed.

You're the real Wonder Woman
with a shield of love and the best
superhero to be written about.

Keeping my Fingers Crossed

People float in their suits, going up to floors to be Mr. Big while they eat their weight in lettuce-wrapped money. Newspaper stories pile on our doorstep for strikers to pick up and stand for something right.

Wheelchair winners pass the broken line as a victory and finally being accepted and seen for the shiny support they needed all these years. Daycare babies wait to see home again as their mothers take care of the beaten eyes that cover their smiley faces to their Facebook followers.

Teens stay in crowds with soaked smoke t-shirts that make it hard to breathe. Trying to find someone alike within the unoriginality pool they swim in daily. Parents in separate beds wish to be the 16-year-olds on the rollercoaster that once made them have fun but now makes them sick just to look over at their aged faces.

Not for each other, they say, as if we're not the same source. Just from two sides of tracks that have crossed over to be at their rightful destination. Midnight oil burns the rough hands that hurt till dawn.

Driving for eternity with blankness on his mind, as that's all he has left to hold, drinking his pain away. We all sleep with our pillow at night with our bodies under the covers. Let's make each other warm tonight if only just once, to have someone with an earful of compassion and all the time in the world for us to hold.

Just Genes

In the 10-year cycle, you come
back like clockwork. The bird
sings its hypocritical song once
more.

As you try to remember my name
but can't seem to find the right
pronunciation. Asking if I still
look like you at all.
Missed birthdays can't be
reversed by false promised gifts
for you to be there.

Have little to write, but I thank
you for giving me life and that
will always be, but I don't need
your jeans.

I only wear skirts and that's all I
need to get by. It's helped me all
my life and I'm doing just fine.

Can't you See

I pray you see that you have more strength than you think. You're a fighter at best. Muhammad Ali could take notes because I know you live secretly in regret.

You're beautiful and smarter than you'll ever know, but you can not see past the wall of disappointment and discomfort that hits you repeatedly when you try.

You think being the crash dummy is a choice, but the car is always unlocked for walking in a new direction.

You think it's lame and you say I won't live anymore if they see me like this now? Trust me, surviving is a mustard seed compared to living your best on top of the mountain.

Make that journey and you won't have to take a second glance ever again.

Thank you "this" Much

Thank you for the supportive stories and advice, seeing that you care.

Thank you for the back rubs, telling us it will be okay, that memory will always stay.

Thank you for your laughter in our darkest and lightest days. Those times are so potent they shine like sun rays.

Lastly, thank you for making this be read, and opening your mind to what needs to be said. You deserve everything you worked so hard for.

Don't return to what was before, because you are so much more. That's for sure.

About the Author

The Author and Ilustrator's name is Alayna Robertson.
She was raised in a Suburban Ohio city, surrounded by the rich Caribbean traditions of her family from Barbados and Trinidad & Tobago.

Alayna's hobbies include genealogy, herbalism, beauty, and artistic pursuits.

Be sure to look out for future publishing from Alayna Robertson.